Bedtime Stories for Children

Bedtime Stories for Children

While every precaution has been taken in the preparation of this book, the publisher assumes no responsibility for errors or omissions, or for damages resulting from the use of the information contained herein.

BEDTIME STORIES FOR CHILDREN

First edition. March 14, 2023.

Copyright © 2023 Liom Liom.

ISBN: 979-8215332252

Written by Liom Liom.

The little star that couldn't sleep

Once upon a time, there was a little star named Twinkle that twinkled high in the sky above the people. Twinkle was a special star because he had a very special job: he had to shine every night and bring joy to the people. But one night Twinkle just couldn't sleep. He felt restless and just couldn't get any rest. He twisted and turned in the sky, wondering why he was so uncomfortable.

Finally, Twinkle decided to take a walk to stretch his legs and maybe find a solution to his problem. He left heaven and landed on earth where he had many adventures. He met a group of animals who took care of him and comforted him. They told him that sometimes it is okay to be uncomfortable and that it is okay to ask for help when you need it.

Twinkle also learned that it was important to get out and have new experiences to solve his problems. He was fascinated by all the new things he discovered on Earth. He saw big forests, meadows full of flowers, and fields full of animals. Twinkle also met many new friends, including a rabbit, a squirrel, and a deer. They all helped him overcome his restlessness and become happy again.

But despite all these adventures, Twinkle still couldn't fall asleep. He missed his family and his job in the sky. So he decided to return and ask the other stars for help. They all gathered around Twinkle and listened intently as he told them about his adventures on Earth. The other stars told him not to worry and that it was okay to be restless sometimes. They reminded him that he had an important job, and that he was bringing joy to people every night.

Twinkle returned to his place in the sky and finally felt content again. He understood that sometimes it was necessary to step out of his comfort zone and have new experiences in order to find a solution to his problems. He learned that it's okay to ask for help, and that there is always someone willing to help.

And so Twinkle shone in the sky every night, spreading joy and happiness to all who saw him. He now knew that it is normal to feel uncomfortable sometimes, but that you can always find a solution if you are willing to step out of your comfort zone.

THE LOST TREASURE IN the garden

Once upon a time, there was a little boy named Max who lived in a small house with a big garden. One day while playing in the garden, Max discovered an old treasure map that had fallen into his hands from an old book in the attic. Max knew immediately that this was the beginning of an exciting adventure.

The map showed Max's garden in secret and mysterious details he had never noticed before. It led him through narrow alleys and across the creek before finally leading to a place in the garden that Max had never seen before.

When Max arrived at the indicated spot, he saw an old tree whose roots seemed to be growing out of the ground. He knew immediately that this must be the place where the lost treasure was buried.

But before Max could lift the treasure, he had to overcome a series of challenges. He climbed the tree to reach the mysterious treasure chest, but it was more difficult than he expected. He slipped and almost fell from the tree, but finally managed to open the box.

The treasure was full of wondrous things like shiny stones, pearls and old coins. Max could hardly believe his luck when he held all the riches in his hands. But he soon realized that the real treasure was that he had mastered the adventure and found the treasure.

Max returned to his house and carefully placed the treasure in a casket, which he hid under his bed. That night, Max fell asleep happy and content, knowing that he had mastered a great adventure.

The moral of the story is to be brave and go on adventures to find treasure. But the greatest treasure often lies in the experience and challenges you overcome along the way.

The adventures of the three little squirrels

Once upon a time there were three little squirrels who lived in a big tree in a dense forest. The squirrels, Lisa, Tim and Max, were best friends and spent the whole day jumping through the branches of the tree and collecting nuts.

One day, however, the three little squirrels heard a loud thump and crack. They looked out of their tree house and saw that a storm was coming. They knew they had to act quickly to protect themselves from the storm.

They decided to go into the forest and find a safe place. But as they walked through the forest, they found a lone, frightened fox being chased by a wild animal. Without hesitation, the three little squirrels decided to help the fox.

They worked together to get the fox to safety, and eventually found an old abandoned tree trunk big enough to shelter them all. They climbed in and held on as the storm raged.

After the storm passed, the three little squirrels crawled out of the log and were relieved to be safe. However, they were very worried about the fox and decided to take him back to the forest where he would be safe.

They helped the fox by feeding him nuts and berries and carrying him on their backs. Finally, they found a quiet place in the forest and left the fox safe and happy.

The three little squirrels returned to their tree house feeling proud of themselves. They realized that it was not only important to take care of themselves, but also to help others when they were in need. And so they lived happily ever after in the forest, always ready to help others when they were needed.

The moral of the story is that it is important to help others and that you often accomplish more when you work together.

No matter how small or big you are, you can always make a difference by helping others and supporting each other.

The Talking Frog at the Pond

Once upon a time there was a small pond where a frog named Felix lived. Felix was no ordinary frog, because he could talk! But Felix was sad, because he had no one to talk to. The other frogs at the pond didn't want to talk to him because they thought he was strange.

One day a little girl named Mia came to the pond. She sat down to watch the frogs and noticed Felix. Felix was amazed that Mia could understand him. They started talking to each other and became fast friends.

Mia told Felix about her adventures at school and Felix told Mia about the things he had experienced at the pond. One day, however, Felix was grabbed by a stork and lifted into the air! Mia was shocked and didn't know what to do.

She thought of Felix and knew she had to help him. She ran to the stork and shouted, "Let go of my friend Felix!" The stork looked at her and said, "Why should I? He's just a frog."

Mia knew she had to act quickly, so she ran back to the pond and called all the frogs together. She explained what had happened and asked for their help to save Felix.

The frogs were skeptical at first, but when they saw how brave Mia was, they decided to help her. Together they climbed a high rock and waited for the stork.

When the stork came back to grab Felix, all the frogs jumped out of hiding and croaked as loud as they could. The stork was so surprised and frightened that he let go of Felix and flew away.

Mia and Felix were relieved and grateful for the frogs' help. Felix was so happy that he had finally found friends who accepted him, whether he could talk or not.

The moral of the story is that it doesn't matter what you look like or if you are different from others. What matters is what is in our heart. Real friends accept us as we are and help us in difficult times.

The secret of the enchanted forest

Once upon a time, there was a little boy named Timmy who wanted nothing more than to have adventures. One day he heard about an enchanted forest that was supposedly full of secrets and adventures. Timmy decided to explore the forest.

When he entered the forest, Timmy noticed that it looked different from any other forest he had seen before. The trees were taller and denser, and it seemed as if they were alive. Timmy couldn't shake the feeling that he was being watched.

Suddenly he heard a soft whisper and followed the sound to a tree stump. There he found a little girl named Lilly, who seemed to be alone and scared. Lilly told him that she was looking for a cure for her sick mother and was hopelessly lost.

Timmy decided to help Lilly and together they set off in search of the cure. They followed a secret path that led them deep into the forest and finally came upon a clearing.

There stood a tree so tall that it seemed to touch the sky. At its base was a hollow from which came a faint glow. Timmy and Lilly ventured into the cave and found a potion that promised to cure Lilly's mother.

When they brought the potion out of the cave, they were surprised by a vicious warlock who wanted to take it from them. But Timmy and Lilly were brave and worked together to defeat the warlock and bring the potion back safely.

As they left the forest, Timmy noticed that the trees no longer seemed alive and the sun was shining again. He asked Lilly what they had done to enchant the forest. Lilly replied, "It was your courage and determination that changed the forest. You proved that you were willing to fight for what was right."

The moral of the story is that courage and determination can help us overcome any obstacle. When we stand up for what is right and help others, we can become heroes ourselves.

The Journey to the Moon

Once upon a time, there was a little girl named Mia who dreamed of traveling to the moon. One night she saw the full moon in the sky and decided that she had had enough of just dreaming and that it was time to start her journey.

Mia decided to build a rocket that would take her to the moon. She gathered all the materials she needed and started building the rocket. It was hard work, but she didn't give up. Finally, the rocket was ready, and Mia prepared for her trip to the moon.

As she climbed into the rocket and began the countdown, she felt a mixture of excitement and fear. The rocket took off and flew higher and higher until it finally reached the moon.

When Mia landed on the moon, she was amazed at the beauty of the planet and the absence of gravity. She jumped and danced on the moon as if she could fly. Suddenly, she noticed a little alien friend who looked sad. Mia asked what was wrong and the little alien told her that he was not able to find his way home.

Mia decided to help him and the two headed back to Earth. While they were flying back, the rocket was hit by an asteroid and damaged. But Mia and the alien worked together and managed to repair the rocket and land safely on Earth.

Mia learned that achieving a goal is not easy, but with perseverance, determination, and cooperation, we can accomplish anything we set our minds to. She also learned that it is important to help others in need and to never give up, even when things get tough.

Mia was happy to be back on Earth, but she knew that her adventures in space would always be on her mind and that she was ready to embark on whatever journey lay ahead.

The brave mouse and the hungry cat

In a small village lived a mouse named Max. Max was not like other mice - he was brave and curious and loved to have new adventures. One day, as Max was walking through the forest, he heard the growl of a hungry tomcat.

Max knew it was dangerous to encounter a hungry cat, but he couldn't help himself and decided to help the cat. He quietly crept up to the cat and asked, "What's wrong? Why are you so hungry?"

The cat told Max that he hadn't found food in days and that he was starving. Max, not wanting the cat to die, decided to help him. He led the cat to a farm where they found a barn full of grains and seeds.

Max and the cat ate together and shared their food. The cat was so grateful for Max's help that he decided to teach him how to sneak through the forest and hide from enemies.

Max learned quickly and became more and more brave and skillful. One day the village was attacked by a gang of hungry rats who stole all the food supplies. Max knew he had to act. With the help of the cat and other animals of the forest, Max set a trap for the rats.

When the rats fell into the trap, the village was saved. Max became the hero of the village and all the animals of the forest celebrated him as a brave and courageous hero.

Max learned that courage and helpfulness are always rewarded and that one should offer help even when it is dangerous. He also learned that friendships can come from the most unexpected places.

The search for the missing teddy bear

Once upon a time, there was a little girl named Mia who had lost her teddy bear that she had had since she was born. She had always had him with her and he was her best friend.

Mia searched her entire house, but her teddy bear was nowhere to be found. She asked her parents and siblings, but no one had seen him. Mia was very sad and decided to look for her teddy bear.

She started her search in the park where she had often played with her teddy bear. But there was no trace of him. Then she remembered the river where she had fed ducks with her teddy bear. But again, her teddy bear was nowhere to be found.

Mia did not give up and asked other children in the park if they had seen her teddy bear. One boy told her that he had seen a bear that had climbed into a tree.

Mia ran to the tree and looked up, but she couldn't see her teddy bear. Then she heard a soft whimpering sound and saw that her teddy bear was stuck between the branches of the tree.

Mia called for help, but no one was around. She had to act herself. With a lot of courage and determination, she climbed the tree and freed her teddy bear. She was very relieved and happy to have found him.

On the way back home, Mia realized that she would never let her teddy bear out of her sight again and that she would cherish him even more than before. She also learned that through persistence and courage, she can accomplish almost anything.

The moral of the story is that we often don't appreciate things until we have lost them. It is also important to know that through persistence and courage, you can accomplish almost anything if you really want it.

The day the rainbow disappeared

It was a day like any other in a small village at the foot of a mountain. The sun was shining, the birds were chirping and people were going about their work. But suddenly something strange happened - the rainbow disappeared! The sky became gray and dreary.

The villagers were worried and wondered what could have happened. The children were especially sad because the rainbow was their favorite sight. They decided to find out what had happened and bring back the rainbow.

They met at the foot of the mountain and began their journey. The landscape became more and more gloomy and it started to rain. But the children did not give up. They climbed higher and higher up the mountain until they came to the edge of a cliff.

There they met a small, frightened bird who explained to them that the rainbow had been stolen by an evil wizard. The wizard had kept the rainbow in a hidden castle, and the only way to get it back was to defeat the wizard.

The children decided to take the bird with them and search for the castle. After a while, they came to an old, dilapidated castle. They sneaked inside and found the wizard guarding the rainbow.

The children bravely fought the wizard and with the help of the little bird and their determination, they managed to defeat him and bring back the rainbow. The sun broke through the clouds again and a new, beautiful rainbow appeared in the sky.

The villagers were overjoyed and celebrated the children as heroes. The children learned that courage and cooperation can overcome anything, even the evillest wizard. They also understood that the rainbow cannot be taken for granted and that we should enjoy the little things in life.

The moral of the story is that it is important to believe in ourselves and our abilities and to work together to overcome difficulties. We should also enjoy and appreciate the little things in life.

The story of the friendly ghost

Once upon a time there was a friendly ghost named Kasper who lived in an old castle. Kasper was not a creepy ghost who spread fear and terror. On the contrary, he liked to help others and be there for them.

One day a family visited the castle and their children were afraid of ghosts. Kasper decided to help the children and show them that ghosts can also be friendly. He followed them around the castle and made doors creak, made shadows appear and made scary noises.

The children were very scared, but Kasper quickly found a way to calm them down. He appeared to them as a friendly ghost and explained that he just wanted to play. The children quickly realized that Kasper was a nice ghost and they began to make friends with him.

Kasper also showed the children some secret ways and hidden treasures in the castle for them to discover. The children had so much fun with Kasper that they almost forgot they were ever afraid of ghosts.

At the end of the day, the children said goodbye to Kasper and thanked him for the exciting day. Kasper was happy that he was able to show the children that ghosts can also be friendly.

The moral of the story is that you should never judge someone without knowing them. Ghosts can be friendly too and it is important to stay open and curious to make new friends.

The discovery of the secret tree house

Once upon a time there was a group of children named Tom, Lucy and Max. They were best friends and loved to play in the forest. One day, while roaming deep in the forest, they discovered something incredible - a tree house they had never seen before.

They excitedly ran to the tree house and climbed up the ladder. When they reached the top, they were amazed at what they saw. The tree house was decorated with pillows, blankets, and lights. There were books, toys, and even a little kitchen!

The children spent the whole afternoon in the tree house and had a wonderful time. When the sun went down, they decided to go back home. But when they turned around to climb down the ladder, they noticed that it was no longer there!

The children were scared and confused, but then they heard a voice coming from the tree house. It was the friendly owner of the tree house, an older man named Henry. He had removed the ladder to make sure no one would enter his tree house unexpectedly.

Henry explained to the children that he had built the tree house when he was a child himself and had used it as a retreat ever since. However, he had always kept it a secret so that no one would find it. But when he saw the children happy and respectful with his tree house, he decided to share it with them.

The children were grateful and promised never to damage or disturb the tree house. From that day on, they met every day in the tree house to play, learn and have adventures. They also learned the importance of respecting secrets and not sharing confidential information.

And so ends our story of Tom, Lucy, and Max discovering the secret tree house and making a wonderful friend. It reminds us that sometimes there are little secrets that should be kept, and that we should always be respectful and kind when we find something special. Good night!

The adventure on the mysterious island

Once upon a time, a group of friends set out for an island that they had heard was full of adventure and mystery. The friends were very excited and packed everything they needed for the adventure.

When they reached the island, they came across a cave hidden deep in the forest. The friends sensed that there was something special here and decided to explore the cave. After climbing through a narrow alley, they came to a large room where an old book lay on a pedestal.

The friends flipped through the pages and found a map that led to a secret treasure on the island. Without hesitation, the friends set out to find the treasure.

They followed the map through the forest and across a bridge to a small island. There they found a chest that was locked with a chain. Suddenly a man appeared and said, "You will never get this treasure!".

The friends were brave and were not intimidated. They fought the man and after a hard struggle they managed to open the chest. Inside they found a map to another secret place on the island.

They followed the map and came to a cave. Inside they found a beautiful treasury full of gold and jewels. The friends were very happy and decided to divide the treasure among themselves.

But then they realized that what they had done was wrong. They had fought and quarreled to gain wealth instead of valuing friendship and togetherness. They decided to leave the treasure behind and enjoy the beauty of the island and its nature instead.

The friends returned home filled with happiness and wisdom about the true value of friendship and nature. They told their friends and families about their adventure and the lessons they had learned, agreeing that it was the best adventure of their lives.

And so ends our story, which shows that friendship and cohesion are the true adventure to be discovered.

THE ENCHANTED MAGIC wand

Once upon a time there was a little girl named Mia who found a magic wand. She was so excited that she tried it out, but nothing happened. Disappointed, she put the wand in her pocket and went into the forest to play.

There she met her friends, the rabbits Dwarf and Lenny. They were playing tag, hide and seek, when suddenly they came across an old man who lived in a dilapidated house.

He told them about an enchanted garden where there were wondrous flowers and plants. The garden was guarded by an evil witch who captured all the children who went inside. But Mia had an idea. She would use the magic wand to defeat the witch and save the garden.

The children made their way to the garden and found it in a sad state. The flowers and plants had withered and the animals were gone. Suddenly the wicked witch appeared and captured the children.

But Mia had a surprise for them. She pulled the magic wand out of her pocket and spoke the magic formula. The wand came to life and shot a powerful ball of energy at the witch, who vanished into thin air.

The enchanted garden began to recover and became a beautiful place full of life and color. The children enjoyed the garden and thanked Mia for her bravery.

The moral of the story is that it is important to be brave and stand up for what you believe in. Sometimes it just takes a little magic to change things for the better.

The little monster who was afraid

Once upon a time there was a little monster named Max who was afraid of everything. He was afraid of loud noises, big animals, and even his own shadow. One day Max decided he had enough of his fear and he decided to face his fears.

He decided to go on an adventure to overcome his fear. He was wandering through the forest where he heard a loud noise. His heart was racing, but he decided to go closer to find out what it was. To his surprise, he found a small bird tangled in a branch. Max gathered all his courage and helped the bird to get free. The bird flew to freedom and Max suddenly felt proud of himself.

Next, Max encountered a big bear that was in trouble. The bear had fallen into a lake and could not swim. Max didn't hesitate and helped the bear get to shore. The bear thanked him and Max felt even braver.

Finally, Max met a small rabbit that was running away from a big shadow. Max realized that the shadow was just from a tree and told the hare not to worry. The hare was grateful and told Max the way home.

Max finally returned to his home and was proud of himself. He had overcome his fear and realized that by being brave and helping others, you can overcome your fears. And from that day on, Max was no longer afraid of big animals, loud noises, or his own shadow.

The moral of the story is that it's okay to be afraid, but it's also important to have the courage to face your fears and help others.

The rescue of the lost kitten

It was a beautiful day in the garden when the three friends, Tim, Lena and Max, discovered a little kitten. It was obviously lost and meowing fearfully. The children decided to help the kitten and bring it back to its family.

But they did not know where the kitten belonged. So they set out to look for clues all over the garden. They asked the birds, the bees and the butterflies if they had seen the kitten, but no one had.

The children didn't give up and kept searching when suddenly they heard a meow from a distance. They followed the sound and finally came to a corner of the garden where they saw the kitten up a tree. It was meowing so loudly that it seemed almost impossible to get it down.

Max, the tallest of the three, climbed the tree and tried to reach the kitten. But when he almost had it, he slipped and fell to the ground. He had hurt himself and could not get up.

Tim and Lena were worried and didn't know what to do. Then Lena remembered that her father worked nearby and could let him know. He came quickly and took Max to the hospital where he was treated.

In the meantime, Lena found the kitten in the tree and returned it safely to its family. Max quickly recovered from his injury and was very grateful for the help of his friends.

The children learned that it is important to help others, even when it can be difficult. They were proud that they had helped the lost kitten and that as friends they will always be there for each other.

And so they fell asleep thinking that tomorrow they would go on adventures together again.

The story of the brave knight and the princess

Once upon a time there was a brave knight named Max who lived in a kingdom full of adventures. One day he heard about a beautiful princess who had been kidnapped by a nasty dragon. Max knew he had to help and set out to rescue the princess.

He crossed forests, forded rivers, and even pushed through a fog that blocked his vision. Finally, he reached the dragon's tower, where he fought the dangerous enemy. The dragon spat fire and lashed out with its tail, but Max was brave and clever. He distracted the dragon until finally he was able to defeat it with a skillful sword thrust.

The princess was saved and Max was hailed as a hero. But before he returned to his kingdom, he taught the princess how to defend herself so that she could take better care of herself in the future. She thanked him for his help and promised never to give up, even if the challenges seemed difficult.

Max returned to his kingdom, where he was celebrated as a great hero. He told everyone about his adventure and emphasized the importance of being brave and courageous in order to succeed in difficult situations.

The moral of this story is that each of us, no matter how small or weak, can make a difference and help others. We should always fight for our beliefs and never be discouraged by difficulties or obstacles.

The adventure in space

Once upon a time there was a group of children who dreamed of adventures and discoveries. One day they discovered an old spaceship sitting in an abandoned hangar. The children were excited and decided to investigate the spaceship and see if it still worked.

They quickly found out that the spaceship did indeed still work and decided to take a trip into space. They named the spaceship "Adventurers" and began to prepare for their trip.

The children worked hard and trained for weeks to be ready for the trip. They learned how to pilot the spaceship, how to deal with zero gravity, and how to survive in a space suit.

Finally, the big day arrived. The children climbed into the spaceship and launched it. They were excited and nervous at the same time as they flew through space.

They quickly discovered that space was full of wonder and mystery. They saw stars and planets they had never seen before and met strange alien creatures that were friendly.

But suddenly the children found themselves in a dangerous asteroid belt. They had to act quickly to avoid being hit. They worked together to maneuver the spaceship safely through the belt, and eventually managed to get away without any damage.

After many days in space, the children finally returned to Earth. They were proud of themselves and happy that they had been so brave and smart.

The moral of the story is that if you work hard and work together, you can accomplish anything you set your mind to. Even if things get difficult, you should not give up and always keep fighting.

The discovery of the hidden castle

Once upon a time, a group of adventurers set out to find a hidden castle that they had heard about in an old legend. The legend said that a powerful treasure was hidden in the castle and whoever would find it would be rich forever.

The adventurers set out, crossing forests and mountains and fighting dangerous animals. After many days of adventure and danger, they finally reached the hidden castle.

They searched the castle from top to bottom, but found no treasure. Instead, they came across a little girl sitting alone in a room crying. The girl told them that she had been separated from her family and had been living alone in the castle ever since.

The adventurers decided to help the girl and together they searched for the way out of the castle. In the process, they came across an evil wizard who was holding the girl captive and wanted to use her for his own benefit.

The adventurers fought the wizard and freed the girl. Together they made their way back to civilization.

On their way back, they learned from the villagers that the treasure from the legend had never existed and that the wizard was using the castle to capture innocent people and keep them as his slaves.

The adventurers understood that sometimes it is more important to help others than just to seek wealth. And so they decided to take the girl into their family and make sure that she would never have to be alone again.

The moral of the story is that helping others is more important than just striving for wealth and personal gain. Cooperation and cohesion can move mountains in difficult situations.

The magic potion that can change everything

Once upon a time, there was a little boy named Max who got lost in a forest. He ran and ran until he discovered an old castle. As he approached the castle, he heard a strange noise. It came from a small room that was locked. Curious as he was, Max searched for a key. Finally, he found one hidden under a flowerpot. When he entered the room, he discovered a potion. A note on the potion said, "This potion can change everything." Max couldn't believe it and decided to try the potion.

He went back to the forest and observed a flower. He poured the potion over the flower and it began to grow and grow until it was as tall as a tree. Then he tried it on a snail, which turned into a turtle. Max was thrilled and thought about what else he could change.

But soon he realized that it could be dangerous to play around with such a powerful potion. He decided to go back to the castle and hide the potion again so that no one would be harmed.

On the way to the castle, Max met a sad frog. The frog told him that he had always dreamed of being a king, but he was just a simple frog. Max decided to help the frog and gave him some of the magic potion. The frog took a big sip and suddenly something began to change. His eyes lit up and his crown grew. He became a true king.

Max now understood that it is not about changing himself, but about helping others to fulfill their dreams. He returned to the castle and hid the potion again, but this time with a different note: "This potion can change everything, but only if it is used to help others."

Max returned home happy and satisfied and told his family and friends about his adventure and the discovery of the potion that can change everything. They were impressed and proud of him.

Max learned that it's not just about the power of a potion, but the responsibility that comes with that power. One should have the power to help others and never forget what is really important in life.

The journey through time

Once upon a time, there was a little girl named Emma who had always wondered what it would be like to live in the past. One day, she found a recipe in an old book for a magical potion that would allow her to travel through time.

Emma was so excited that she immediately decided to brew the potion. She gathered all the ingredients she needed and began to prepare the potion. After a few hours, the potion was finally ready. Emma drank it and immediately felt herself being thrown back in time.

When she woke up, she was in a village in the Middle Ages. The people were all dressed in medieval clothes and riding around on horses. Emma was completely fascinated and decided to explore the village.

She met a nice man named Thomas who explained that she was in the year 1345. Emma couldn't believe it and asked Thomas if he could show her around the village.

As she traveled through the village, Emma learned how people lived back then. She saw how they prepared their food, how they dressed, and how they talked. It was like traveling back in time.

But suddenly Emma noticed that something was wrong. Some of the villagers were sick and there was no medicine to help them. Emma knew she had to do something.

She remembered an old trick that her grandmother had taught her. She took some herbs and prepared a healing tea. She gave it to the sick villagers and soon they felt better.

The people in the village were so grateful for Emma's help that they decided to give her a reward. But Emma did not want a reward. She just wanted to help and do something good.

When she drank the potion, she returned to the present. Emma was happy and satisfied that she could help the people of the Middle Ages and that she could do something good.

The moral of this story is that it is important to help others when they are in need. No matter what time we live in, we should always do our best to help others and make the world a better place.

THE ADVENTURES OF THE talking animals in the forest

Once upon a time there was a forest where many animals lived. One day they noticed that they could all talk! The animals were amazed, but soon they realized that they had a common task. A group of beavers had dammed up the river and polluted the water, which was harming the animals in the forest.

The animals decided to act together and solve the problem. A brave bear, a clever owl, a shrewd fox and many other animals joined together to tackle the problem. Together they built a dam to make the river flow again, and they cleaned the water.

But when they built the dam, they came into conflict with the beavers. The beavers did not want their work to be destroyed and fought back against the animals. However, the talking animals were determined to restore the river and worked hard to remove the dam.

In the end, the animals succeeded in making the river flow freely again and cleaning up the water. The beavers finally realized the importance of sticking together and apologized to the other animals. From then on, all the animals worked together to protect and preserve their forest.

The moral of the story is that cohesion and cooperation are very important. If we act together, we can accomplish a lot and protect our environment.

The Enchanted Garden

In a small village lived a girl named Mia. One day she discovered a secret door in her backyard that led to a beautiful garden. There she saw the most beautiful flowers and trees she had ever seen. Suddenly, she noticed that some of the flowers and trees were moving. When she looked closer, she discovered that they were inhabited by tiny fairies and elves.

The fairies and elves were very friendly and showed Mia their garden. But they also told her about an evil wizard who had put a curse on their garden. Since then, the fairies and elves were not allowed to leave their garden to get new plants and flowers.

Mia decided to help the fairies and elves and break the wizard's curse. She agreed to go in search of the wizard and defeat him. The fairies and elves were grateful for her help and gave her a magic key that would show her the way to the wizard's castle.

Mia set out on her mission and followed the magic key through a dark forest and across a dangerous river. Finally, she came to a large fortress surrounded by a wall. Mia opened the gate with the magic key and entered the castle.

There she met the evil wizard who confronted her with a magic staff. But Mia did not give up and fought against him. She ducked skillfully, dodged his attacks and finally managed to snatch the staff from him.

When she took the staff in her hand, something strange happened. The staff began to glow and swing. Mia realized that it was the staff of the garden, which had the power to break the curse.

With the staff, Mia returned to the garden of fairies and elves and cast a spell. Immediately the withered plants and trees blossomed again and the garden shone in full splendor. The fairies and elves danced with joy and thanked Mia.

But Mia had one more surprise for them. She gave the fairies and elves the garden's staff and explained that from now on they could use it to keep their garden always beautiful and healthy. The fairies and elves were touched and thanked Mia from their hearts.

The next morning, Mia woke up and looked into her garden. She was relieved and happy to see that the garden was still in full bloom and the fairies and elves were happy. She realized that it is important to help others and that good deeds are always rewarded.

THE STORY OF THE FLYING elephant

Once upon a time there was a little elephant named Ellie. Ellie was different from other elephants because he had something that none of his fellow elephants had: wings! More specifically, he had two beautiful, colorful wings that allowed him to fly. Ellie loved to fly, he flew as often and as far as he could, discovering many wonderful places along the way.

One day Ellie heard about a magical place called "The Garden of Wishes". This garden was guarded by a fairy who granted a wish to everyone who visited it. Ellie was excited and decided to find the Garden of Wishes. He asked other animals if they knew the garden, but no one could help him.

One day he met an old bird named Victor who knew the garden. Victor told him that the garden was far away and he had to fly over many dangerous mountains and rivers to get there.

Ellie was afraid, but he wanted to fulfill his greatest wish and decided to dare to go.

Ellie flew over dangerous canyons and rivers and fought against strong winds. But he did not give up and kept flying until he finally reached the Garden of Wishes. The fairy greeted him and asked for his wish. Ellie did not hesitate for a moment and asked that all the animals he had met should be able to fly.

The fairy smiled and granted his wish. Ellie returned to his friends and told them about his adventure and that they could all fly now. They could hardly believe it, but when they looked around, all the animals had colorful wings like Ellie.

Ellie was happy and proud of his feat. He had fulfilled his dream and helped others fulfill their dreams. The moral of the story is to be brave and follow your dreams even if it seems difficult, and to care about others and help them fulfill their dreams.

The Adventure on Pirate Island

Once upon a time, there was a little girl named Emma. One day her father told her about a mysterious pirate island where a fabulous treasure was supposedly hidden. Emma was thrilled and decided to find this island. Together with her best friend Max and her cat Luna, she set off.

They sailed through dangerous waters and fought against wild storms. Finally, they reached the island and started searching for the treasure. But they were not alone. A gang of dangerous pirates also had the goal of finding the treasure.

Emma and her friends had to hide and hide from the pirates. When they finally came across the treasure map, they followed it through a series of dangerous traps and obstacles. Finally, they reached the place where the treasure was hidden.

But before they could reach it, they were attacked by the pirates. A wild brawl broke out and it seemed that the friends would lose. But then a group of friendly pirates suddenly appeared and helped them defeat the attackers.

In the end, they found the treasure, but Emma and her friends decided not to keep it. Instead, they shared it with the friendly pirates and promised to always be friends.

The moral of the story was that friendship is more important than wealth and that you should always help others if you can. Emma and her friends returned home happy, knowing they had had an adventure they would never forget.

The discovery of the secret waterfall

Once upon a time there was a small village surrounded by a high mountain. No one knew what lay beyond the mountain, but everyone had heard that there was a secret waterfall. However, this waterfall was very difficult to reach because there were many dangers on the way. But that didn't stop a group of brave children from trying to find the waterfall.

One day the children met on the outskirts of the village and decided that they would find the secret waterfall. They knew they would be embarking on a dangerous journey, but they were willing to take the risk.

The children set off and followed an old path that led deep into the forest. The forest was dark and scary, but the children kept going. They crossed rivers and hiked over mountains. After many hours, they finally reached a steep slope. They had to be careful not to slip, but in the end they arrived safely.

And there, deep in the heart of the forest, they found the secret waterfall. It was a spectacular sight. The waterfall plunged from a high cliff into a beautiful pool. The pool was surrounded by a dense green forest that blocked the sun's rays and bathed the place in a magical light.

But that wasn't all. The children also discovered a secret cave behind the waterfall. They entered it carefully and found an ancient treasure. It was a suitcase full of gold coins, precious stones and valuable antiques.

The children were thrilled, but they also knew that they could not keep the treasure. They decided to bring it back to the village and share it with the community. It was a difficult journey, but they made it safely back to the village and brought the treasure to the mayor.

The mayor was very proud of the children and declared that they had made a great contribution to the community. He divided the treasure equally and used the money to improve the village. There were new schools, parks and roads. Not only had the children discovered the secret waterfall, but they had also helped make their village a better place.

The moral of the story is that there are always risks in discovering new things. But if you work hard and stick together, you can accomplish amazing things while helping others.

The talking parrot at the zoo

It was a sunny day at the zoo when the children Max and Lena met a special parrot. This parrot was different from all the other parrots at the zoo - he could talk! The parrot named Sammy was very friendly and invited Max and Lena to visit him in his cage.

Sammy told them about his adventure when he was brought to the zoo from his original home in a faraway country. He missed his family and his freedom, but he had also made new friends, including some other parrots.

Suddenly, Max and Lena heard a noise from a neighboring cage. It was a little monkey named Coco who had hurt himself and needed urgent help. Sammy, the talking parrot, had an idea. He knew where to find the vet at the zoo and asked Max and Lena to follow him.

Together with Sammy, the children set out to get the vet. On the way, they encountered various animals such as giraffes, zebras, and even a lion. Sammy knew the zoo like the back of his hand and showed the children the fastest way to the vet.

When they reached the vet, they explained the situation with Coco. The vet examined the little monkey and gave him the necessary treatment. Coco recovered quickly and was soon back with his friends in his cage.

Max and Lena were so grateful for the help of Sammy, the talking parrot. Sammy told them that he loved helping them and that he was very happy that they had become friends.

The children spent the rest of the day with Sammy, who told them a lot about the zoo and its inhabitants. They promised to visit Sammy every day to continue learning from him.

At the end of the day, Max and Lena learned that it doesn't matter how different we are. We can always make friends and help each other if we work together. They thanked Sammy for the adventure and the valuable lesson.

And Sammy was glad that he had made new friends who visited him and helped him when he needed it. It was a beautiful day at the zoo and a day they would always remember.

The search for the lost butterfly

Once upon a time there was a little girl named Mia. She loved to play and explore outside in nature. One day she spotted a beautiful butterfly with bright blue wings. She was following him through the forest when suddenly he disappeared into a thick bush. Mia tried to find it, but the butterfly had disappeared.

Sadly, Mia went back to her house, but she couldn't get the thought of the lost butterfly out of her mind. She decided to go searching the next day with her friend Ben. Together they searched the forest and finally found the bush where the butterfly had disappeared. But they didn't find it.

Mia did not give up. She knew the butterfly had to be somewhere. So she asked the animals in the forest for help. A squirrel told them about an enchanted lake where magical butterflies were said to live. Without hesitation, Mia and Ben set off for the lake.

Once there, they saw a beautiful world full of butterflies in different colors and patterns. But they couldn't find the blue butterfly. Then suddenly they heard a little voice: "Can you help me?" It was the butterfly! It had hurt itself and couldn't fly.

Mia and Ben carefully tied the butterfly's wing and carried it back to the forest. There was a medicinal plant there that could help the butterfly. They found the plant and took it to the butterfly. After they helped it, it could fly again.

The two children were overjoyed to have saved the butterfly. But they also learned an important lesson: you should never give up when you have a goal, and you should always be ready to help others when they are in need.

And so ended the story of Mia and Ben, who had found and rescued the lost butterfly, learning an important lesson about perseverance and being helpful.

42

The story of the magical fairy

Once upon a time there was a little fairy named Lilli who lived in a forest that was full of wonders and mysteries. Lilli had a special magic that enabled her to bring joy and happiness to people. One day Lilli decided to go on a journey to make new friends and learn more about the world.

On her journey, Lilli met many animals and people, but none of them was as special as the little boy named Max. Max was alone and sad and Lilli felt that he needed her help. She asked him what was wrong and he told her that he was bullied at school.

Lilli knew she had to help Max, so she decided to give him her magic power. She gave him a small magic wand and told him that with this wand he could make all his wishes come true as long as he always stayed positive and kind.

Max couldn't believe it and asked Lilli if she was sure he had this power. Lilli smiled and said, "I believe in you, Max. You have what it takes to perform miracles if you only believe."

Max was thrilled and immediately tried out his new wand. He wished he could find friends who accepted him as he was. And suddenly three animals appeared: a rabbit, a fox, and a squirrel. They said that they wanted to be Max's new friends.

Max was overjoyed and realized that the magic wand really worked. He thanked Lilli for her help and vowed to always be positive and friendly.

Lilli was proud of Max and knew that he would become a true friend to all the animals and people he met. She gave him a kiss on the cheek and flew back to her forest.

And so Max lived happily and full of wonder, always accompanied by his new animal friends and his magic wand. He had learned that faith and kindness were the keys to happiness, and that with a little magic you could achieve anything.

The adventure in fairyland

Once upon a time there was a little girl named Lilly who had a great adventure. One night she dreamed of a land full of fairy tales and magic. She was so excited that she decided to go there.

When she woke up, she found herself in another world. She was in a landscape full of magnificent castles, fairy-tale creatures, and mysterious forests. Lily could hardly believe it, but she had landed in fairyland!

She decided to explore the land and began her journey through the wondrous world. She met friendly fairies, helpful trolls and brave knights. Each of them told her about the dangers that lurked in the fairyland.

Lily was very curious and wanted to learn more about these dangers. She set off for a mysterious castle guarded by an evil wizard. The wizard had put a curse on the land that shrouded everything in darkness.

Lilly dared to sneak into the castle and discovered the evil wizard working on a powerful spell. The spell would shroud the entire fairyland in darkness forever.

Lilly knew she had to do something to stop the wizard. She remembered the stories she had heard on her journey and decided to find a solution.

She returned to the friendly fairies, who gave her a magical item that could lift the evil wizard's spell.

With the magic object, Lilly set out for the wizard's castle. She overcame all obstacles to reach the evil wizard. With a loud scream she smashed the magic object against the wall and the curse was lifted.

Fairyland was saved and it returned to its merry and bright state. The inhabitants of Fairyland thanked Lilly for her bravery and courage.

Lilly returned to the real world feeling happy and proud of her heroic deeds in Fairyland. She learned that courage and determination are important in her world as well, and that if you face your fears, you can always discover something wonderful.

The discovery of the hidden treasure in the desert

Once upon a time, a group of friends went on an exciting journey together into the desert. They wandered for hours through the hot sand until suddenly they discovered a secret entrance to a cave.

They crawled inside and found themselves in a room full of treasures. Gold coins, jewels, and sparkling gems lay everywhere. The friends were overwhelmed by the sight and began to examine the treasures.

But then they heard a deep growl and saw a large scorpion coming towards them. They ran for their lives and soon found themselves in another room. This room was dark and creepy, but they heard a noise and followed it. They found a door that led to another room.

This room was empty except for a huge mirror on the wall. They looked inside and suddenly a man appeared in the mirror saying, "I hid the treasure here many years ago. But the one who finds it must prove that he has a good heart and will use the treasure to help others."

The friends knew they couldn't just keep the treasure for themselves. They wanted to use it to help others and do good. So they set out back to the town to share the treasure and build a school so that the children of the town would have a better future.

The friends knew they had done the right thing and were happy to know they had helped others. Not only had they found the hidden treasure, but they had also found a good heart.

The rescue of the little bird

It was a beautiful day in the forest when Lina and her friends came across a little bird that had fallen from a tree. The bird was scared and could no longer fly. Lina and her friends decided to help the little bird and take care of it.

They built him a little nest and brought him food and water. The little bird was very grateful and quickly began to recover. One day, Lina and her friends decided to release the little bird back into the wild. The little bird flew away and they were happy that they could help him.

But suddenly they heard a loud cawing sound from far away. They followed the sound and discovered a big bird caught in a net. Lina and her friends knew they had to help the big bird.

They worked together and freed the big bird from the net. The big bird was so grateful that he led them to his secret hiding place where he kept a hidden treasure. The friends were amazed and delighted at the same time. The big bird said to them, "This treasure is yours because you helped me".

Lina and her friends were overwhelmed by what they had experienced. They realized that it is important to help others because you never know what rewards life has in store. They decided to share the treasure and donate the money to charity.

And so their adventure in the forest ended with a wonderful lesson: it's always good to help others, because at the end of the day it could lead to an unexpected and generous gift.

The story of the brave dragon

Once upon a time there was a small village that was terrorized by a terrible dragon. The dragon had terrified the villagers by burning down their houses and destroying their fields. No one dared to resist him.

One day, a little boy named Max came to the village. He had heard that the dragon was terrorizing the village and wanted to help. He thought about it for a long time and finally came up with an idea.

He decided to defeat the dragon by giving it something he had never experienced before. He gathered all his friends and built a big attraction, a huge dragon made of straw and wood. They took it to the village square and waited for the real dragon to appear.

When the dragon appeared, he flew straight towards the artificial dragon. But he was surprised when he bumped into the fake dragon and realized it was just a dummy. He landed in the village square and looked around. There he discovered a group of children gathered around him.

Max stepped forward and said, "Oh great dragon, why are you terrorizing this village? What do you get out of it?"

The dragon replied, "I'm hungry and can't find food in the wild."

Then Max had an idea. He offered the dragon that if he stopped terrorizing the village, he would help them find a place where he could find enough to eat.

The dragon was surprised that someone wanted to help him and was willing to make an agreement. Max and his friends led the dragon to a nearby mountain where there were many sheep and goats. The dragon was happy to finally have enough to eat and promised never to bother the village again.

The villagers were relieved that the dragon was finally defeated, and Max and his friends were hailed as heroes. They had proven that ingenuity and kindness can go a long way.

The moral of the story is that you can solve even the seemingly worst problems if you are resourceful and brave enough. Even if it is sometimes difficult, you should always try to be kind and respectful to others, because this can lead to unexpected friendships.

The adventure in the underwater world

Once upon a time, there was a little girl named Mia who dreamed of discovering the wonders of the underwater world. One day she found a magical bracelet that allowed her to breathe underwater.

Excited by the possibility of exploring the underwater world, Mia did not hesitate to jump into the ocean. She saw fish of all colors and sizes and discovered coral reefs so beautiful that it took her breath away.

But suddenly she heard a loud rumbling and growling. A huge octopus appeared and entangled Mia in its tentacles. She struggled desperately to free herself, but the octopus was too strong.

Fortunately, at that moment, two brave dolphins appeared and grabbed the tentacles of the octopus and freed Mia. Gratefully, Mia followed the dolphins and discovered a hidden cave.

There she met an old mermaid who taught her an important lesson about protecting the marine world. She told Mia that everyone has a responsibility to protect the oceans and that every little bit can help.

Mia left the cave with a new awareness and vowed to protect the underwater world. She returned to the shore and picked up the trash that was lying on the beach with her friends.

Since that day, Mia has been a great advocate for the marine world and taught other children the importance of protecting the environment.

The moral of this story is that we all have a responsibility to protect our environment and that even the smallest actions can make a difference.

The discovery of the secret temple

Once upon a time, there was a little boy named Max who had always been passionate about adventure and mystery. One day he found a treasure map that led him to a secret temple he had never heard of. He decided to go on a quest to find out what this temple was all about.

Max wandered through dense jungle and over Rocky Mountains until he finally found the entrance to the temple. The doors were locked, but Max found a way to get inside. As he wandered through the dark corridors of the temple, he noticed that he was not alone. A small, black and white dog followed him every step of the way.

Finally, Max and the dog reached a large room where a huge gem stood on an altar. Max knew immediately that this was the treasure he had been looking for. But before he could take the gem, he heard a deep voice saying, "Only the worthy can receive this treasure."

Max looked around, but could see no one. Then he saw that the little dog was talking to him! The dog explained that he was a magic dog and could help him get the treasure if Max could prove that he was worthy.

Max had to pass a series of tests to prove that he was brave, honest and considerate. Finally, he managed to pass all the tests and the dog turned into a magical bat. With the bat as his guide, Max managed to take the gem and leave the temple safely.

When Max returned home, he realized that the treasure he had found was not only a precious gemstone, but also the friendship and experience he had with the magic dog. He had learned that it is not always about the destination, but also about the way to get there and the people and beings we meet along the way.

Max and the dog remained friends forever, and Max told everyone about his adventure and the lessons he had learned.

The talking monkey in the jungle

Once upon a time there was a little monkey named Timmy who lived in the deep jungle. Timmy was different from the other monkeys. He could talk! But his ability earned him not only admiration, but also envy and resentment.

One day, while Timmy was walking alone in the jungle, he was kidnapped by a group of nasty monkeys. They were jealous of his ability and wanted to force him to teach them how to talk.

Timmy was sad and scared, but he decided not to give up. He waited for an opportunity to escape and one day, when the guards of the group were careless, he took the chance and ran away.

During his escape, he met a wise old monkey who helped him hide and defend himself. Together they had many adventures and Timmy learned how important it is to have friends who support and protect you.

Eventually, Timmy returned to his monkey group, but this time he was respected and admired by everyone because he was brave and smart.

The moral of this story is that it is important to stay true to yourself and not give up, even if you are different from others. It is also significant to surround yourself with the people who will support and protect you and to share your skills and strengths to inspire and motivate others.

The search for the lost key

Once upon a time, there was a little girl named Emma who lived with her family in a big house on the outskirts of town. One day, Emma noticed that the key to her secret diary had disappeared. She had last seen the key in her room, but now it had just disappeared.

Emma searched everywhere in her room and in the rest of the house, but could not find the key. She was very sad because her diary had her deepest secrets and dreams written down. So she decided to look for the key and asked her friends Max and Mia to help her. Together they set out on their search.

First they searched the whole house, but the key was nowhere to be found. Then they went to the park where Emma often played, but again there was no trace of the key. Finally, they decided to go to the nearby forest.

As they were walking in the forest, they suddenly heard a strange noise. They followed the sound and finally came to a hidden pond where a small boat was floating. Emma, Max and Mia got into the boat and rowed to a small island in the middle of the pond.

There they discovered an old tree stump that looked like a gate. When they climbed through the stump, they suddenly found themselves in a secret cave. In the cave there was a box with a note on it that said, "If you are looking for the key to your heart, you will find it here."

Emma, Max and Mia opened the box and inside was a small key that perfectly matched Emma's diary. They were so happy that they danced with joy. They realized that the key they had been looking for was not just an ordinary key, but a symbol of their dreams and wishes.

They returned home and Emma finally opened her diary. She read in it all her thoughts and dreams, and realized that through her search for the key she had learned something very important: that sometimes it is difficult to find what you are looking for, but you have to persevere and believe in yourself.

Emma decided never to give up when she was looking for something that was important to her. She knew that she always had the courage and determination to achieve her goals, and she knew that her friends would always be by her side to help her.

Thus ended the story of Emma, Max and Mia and their adventure to find the lost key. They realized that sometimes the adventure itself is more important than the goal, and that friendship and cohesion are the keys to success.

The story of the mysterious pyramid

Once upon a time, there was a little boy named Max who was always excited about adventure. One day he heard about a mysterious pyramid in Egypt that supposedly housed an incredible treasure. Without hesitation, Max set off for it.

When he arrived in Egypt, he met an old man named Ali who told him about the dangers of the jungle. But Max was brave and determined and set out anyway, accompanied by his faithful dog Rex.

They fought wild animals and overcame dangerous obstacles. Finally, they reached the pyramid and found the entrance. But suddenly they heard a strange noise and faced a horde of tomb robbers.

Max and Rex had to use all their skills to escape the tomb robbers and enter the pyramid. They found a secret chamber and discovered a treasure even bigger than anything they had ever imagined.

But when they went to take the treasure, they were captured by the mysterious pyramid. They were trapped and did not know how to escape.

At that moment, a wise old man appeared and said, "You have found the treasure, but you have also learned that wealth alone is not everything. It is courage that counts and the desire to achieve the impossible. You've proven that you're willing to fight for what you want and that you won't give up, even when the challenges are great."

Max and Rex realized that it wasn't the treasure that made the adventure worth it, but the journey itself. They returned home enriched by the experience and the knowledge that they could overcome any challenge if only they were brave enough.

The adventure in the magic world

Once upon a time, there was a little girl named Lena who always dreamed of traveling to a magical world full of adventure and wonder. One day, while walking through the forest, she discovered a door that led deep into the ground. Without hesitation, Lena opened the door and fell into a deep hole.

When she woke up, she found herself in a magical world full of twinkling stars and colorful flowers. All around her were talking animals and plants. She met a friendly fox named Felix who explained that she was in the magical world.

Lena and Felix went on an adventure through the magical world to find the magic crystal that was stolen and threatened the peace of the world. They had to fight dangerous creatures and solve difficult puzzles to find the crystal.

Finally, they reached the sinister palace of the evil wizard who had stolen the crystal. They fought against his evil servants and finally defeated the wizard and brought back the crystal.

Lena returned to her own world and was grateful for the adventure she had had. She had learned that life can be full of surprises and adventures if you are brave enough to accept them.

The moral of the story is that you have to be brave to achieve your dreams and have adventures. You should always be ready to take on new challenges and face difficulties to achieve your goals.

The discovery of the hidden valley

Once upon a time there was a little boy named Tim who one day discovered a secret valley. It was hidden behind a high mountain and was surrounded by dense forest. Tim was excited and wanted to learn more about the valley.

When he went deeper into the valley, he found a mysterious cave. He decided to go inside and discovered a magic crystal. When he touched it, he was suddenly surrounded by a bright light and found himself in another world.

In this world he met many friendly beings and adventures that made him overcome his fears and become braver. He also learned that it is important to help others and show cohesion.

After many exciting experiences, Tim finally returned to the real world and decided to share his adventures with his friends and family. They were thrilled and decided to explore the secret valley together.

Through Tim's courage and spirit of discovery, they had an exciting adventure and learned valuable lessons about friendship and cohesion. They also realized that through courage and a spirit of discovery, you can experience many new things that enrich your life.

And so ends our story about Tintin and the Secret Valley, reminding us that there are always new things to discover if you are brave and curious, and that cohesion and friendship will sustain us in all our adventures.

The rescue of the little hedgehog

Once upon a time there was a little hedgehog named Igi who lived in a forest. Igi was very curious and adventurous. One day he decided to leave the forest and explore the world.

Igi wandered all day and all night until he finally arrived at a big road. He was about to cross the road when a loud car drove by and startled him. Igi quickly ran back into the forest and hid.

When he came out again, he was very hungry and tired. He wandered on and came across a field full of berries. But when he went to eat the berries, he saw a big dog growling at him. Igi ran away again and hid under a tree.

But suddenly he heard a small, faint whimper. He followed the sound and found a small hedgehog stuck in a barbed wire fence. Igi knew he had to help.

He bit and scratched at the wire until the little hedgehog was freed. The little hedgehog was very grateful and Igi was proud of himself.

They wandered on together and finally reached a town. In the town lived a man named Mr. Schmitt who had a big garden. Mr. Schmitt had many problems with snails in his garden and was very sad about it.

When Igi and the little hedgehog met Mr. Schmitt, they told him about their trip and how they had helped each other. Mr. Schmitt was impressed by the friendship and helpfulness of the two hedgehogs.

Mr. Schmitt told them about his snail problem and asked for help. Igi and the little hedgehog were willing to help and started to collect the snails and bring them out of the garden.

At the end of the day they were successful and Mr. Schmitt was very happy and grateful. He gave the two hedgehogs something to eat and they spent a night in his garden.

The next day Igi and the little hedgehog returned to the forest. They were very happy and proud of their adventures. They had learned that friendship and helpfulness are very important and that they must stick together in difficult times.

From that day on, Igi was no longer just an adventurous hedgehog, but also a friend who helped others when they were in need.

The story of the magical unicorn

Once upon a time there was a little girl named Lily who always dreamed of unicorns. One day, while she was walking in the forest, she heard a strange noise. It sounded like a soft snort, and when she turned around, she saw a white unicorn standing in front of her.

Lily could hardly believe that she had found a real unicorn! It was beautiful and had silky white fur that sparkled in the sunlight. It looked at her with its big eyes and Lily felt that it wanted to tell her something. But the unicorn couldn't speak.

So Lily decided to play with the unicorn and pet it. The unicorn seemed to enjoy it and Lily noticed that it was very trusting. Eventually, however, she had to go back home and said goodbye to the unicorn.

That night, Lily dreamed of the unicorn and wished she could see it again. The next day, when she went back to the forest, the unicorn was there again! This time it followed her and Lily led it through the forest. They passed a river where the unicorn quenched its thirst, and Lily discovered a hidden waterfall. They were so excited about their adventure that they decided to explore the waterfall.

On the way to the waterfall, they met a fox who was lost. Lily and the unicorn helped him find his way back home. They learned that it is important to help others when they are in trouble.

Finally, they reached the waterfall and discovered something amazing. There on top of the waterfall was a rainbow shining on the ground. Lily and the unicorn stood under the rainbow and something magical happened. The unicorn began to speak!

It explained to Lily that it had chosen her as its friend because she was kind and caring. The unicorn led Lily and the fox to the end of the rainbow, where they found a hidden door in a tree hollow. They opened the door and found a beautiful cave full of sparkling gems and crystals.

There the unicorn explained to Lily that she now had a responsibility to keep the unicorn secret. She couldn't tell everyone about it or the secret would no longer be a secret. She learned that secrets are important and should be protected.

Lily and the unicorn spent the rest of the day together and had lots of fun. When it was time for Lily to go home, she said goodbye to her new friend. She knew that she now had a special connection with unicorns and would always think of this incredible adventure.

The moral of the story is that it is important to be kind and caring, to help others, to protect secrets, and to let your imagination inspire you and have adventures.

The adventure in the snow

It was a cold winter day in the village of animals. The snow covered everything and the temperature was so low that most of the animals stayed in their warm caves or houses. But a little squirrel named Kiki was so excited that she couldn't bear to stay inside. She was eager to discover the beauty of winter and experience something.

So Kiki set off into the snowy forest, hopping from tree to tree, when suddenly she heard a strange noise. It sounded like a call for help. Kiki followed the sound and found a small deer stuck in the snow. It was panicking and couldn't run any further.

Kiki didn't hesitate and helped the deer out of the snow. The deer was so grateful that it confided a little secret to Kiki: there was a secret cave in the forest where a magic crystal was hidden. The crystal had the power to enchant winter and turn everything into a wondrous place.

Kiki was so excited and desperate to find this magic crystal. The little deer helped her find the way to the secret cave. They crossed the forest and finally reached a cave hidden deep in the snow.

When they went inside, they found a crystal that sparkled so beautifully that Kiki immediately fell in love with it. But suddenly they heard footsteps and saw an evil fox following them. The fox had also discovered the crystal and was determined to steal it.

Kiki and the deer knew they had to save the crystal from the fox. Kiki had an idea and challenged the fox to a race in the snow. The fox was so arrogant that he accepted the challenge, not realizing that Kiki and the deer had a clever strategy.

They ran, and while the fox ran fast, Kiki and the deer found a shortcut through the forest and reached the cave before the fox. They took the crystal and ran away as fast as they could.

When the fox finally arrived, he found the cave empty and Kiki and the deer were nowhere to be seen. He was so angry that he screamed and stomped on the ground.

Kiki and the deer brought the magic crystal back to the village of the animals and transformed the winter into a beautiful place full of beauty and joy. The animals were so grateful for Kiki's courage and determination to save the crystal and enchant Winter.

The moral of this story is that with courage and determination, you can accomplish anything, even if it looks difficult. Sometimes you can also overcome obstacles through clever strategies and teamwork.

The discovery of the secret mountain

Once upon a time there was a little boy named Tom who was very adventurous. One day he heard about a secret mountain where a treasure was supposedly hidden. Tom couldn't resist and set out to find the mountain.

After several days of searching through dense forests and over high mountains, he finally found the secret mountain. But before he could find the treasure, he had to climb up a steep path. Tom climbed and climbed until he finally reached the top of the mountain.

There he found a cave and when he ran inside, he saw a beautiful diamond standing on a pedestal. But suddenly he heard a growl and saw a big bear threatening him. Tom was very frightened, but he knew he had to distract the bear somehow to get to the diamond.

He threw some fruits and nuts on the ground and the bear ran to eat them. At that moment, Tom quickly grabbed the diamond and ran out of the cave. The bear noticed and chased him. Tom ran and ran until he finally climbed a tree. The bear could not reach him and finally gave up.

Tom was relieved and happy that he had found the diamond. But when he held it in his hand, he realized that the real treasure he had found was not the diamond, but the adventure he had had.

Tom had learned that life is not only about material things, but also about experiences and challenges that make us stronger and braver. And so he returned home with this knowledge and a new sense of self.

The moral of the story is that in life it is important to seek new adventures and overcome challenges in order to grow and develop. Sometimes we have to take risks to achieve what we really want, but it is worth it to have valuable experiences in the end.

The talking bear in the forest

Once upon a time, there was a little girl named Mia who went for a walk in the forest. When she was deep in the forest, she suddenly heard a loud humming sound. She followed the sound and discovered a big, brown bear.

The bear was talking to her! "Hello, little girl. What are you doing here alone in the forest?" he asked.

Mia was surprised that the bear could talk. "I'm going for a walk," she answered.

The bear looked sad. "I'm lost and I can't find my way home. Can you help me?" he asked.

Mia felt sorry for the bear and agreed to help him. Together they searched the forest for the right way. They climbed over logs and steep hills and crossed streams and ditches.

After several hours, they finally found the path that led the bear to his home. The bear was very happy and grateful for Mia's help.

"Thank you so much for helping me," the bear said. "I am very grateful to you. How can I thank you?"

Mia thought for a moment and finally replied, "I don't need a reward. But I would appreciate it if you would always be kind to the animals in the forest and respect them. They are just as important as we humans."

The bear nodded and promised to stick to it. Mia and the bear said goodbye and she returned home.

That night, Mia learned that you should always help others when you can, and that it is important to be respectful and kind to all living things.

The search for the lost treasure in the city

Once upon a time, a group of friends went on an exciting treasure hunt in the city. They heard stories about a secret treasure hidden somewhere in the streets of the city. The friends were very excited and decided to find it.

They searched all the places they knew: the park, the river, the playground and many other places. They looked under every rock and behind every corner, but they found nothing.

One afternoon they decided to ask an old man for help. He told them a story about a hidden treasure in an old abandoned mansion on the outskirts of town. The friends were thrilled and immediately set out.

When they reached the villa, they saw that the gate was locked. They looked for another entrance and finally found a window that was open. They climbed in and started searching the rooms.

When they reached the last room, they found an old chest. They opened it and found a map inside that led to another treasure. The friends were excited and set out to find the next treasure.

They followed the map through the streets of the town and finally it led to a hidden garden where they found a chest full of gold and gems.

The friends were so happy that they hugged each other with joy. They decided to divide the gold among themselves and donate some of it to the poor.

They learned that it is not only about finding treasure, but also about sharing the joy and happiness. And so they decided that their most valuable learning from this adventure was that they should work together and share to make everyone happy.

And with that thought in mind, the friends fell asleep happy, knowing that together they could accomplish anything.

Impressum

LIOM LIOM
AUF DER HÖH 13A
35447 REISKIRCHEN
KONTAKT
E-MAIL: sl350sl@gmx.de

Don't miss out!

Visit the website below and you can sign up to receive emails whenever Liom Liom publishes a new book. There's no charge and no obligation.

https://books2read.com/r/B-A-AOUW-WLQGC

BOOKS 2 READ

Connecting independent readers to independent writers.

Did you love *Bedtime Stories for Children*? Then you should read *Bedtime Stories for the Little Ones*[1] by Liom Liom!

Experience the power of imagination with our new e-book, "40 Bedtime Stories for Kids." This book will take kids on a world of adventure, fun and magic and make sure they fall asleep peacefully every night. From brave dragons and brave princesses to funny animals and mysterious creatures, each story is unique and will delight children. This e-book is the perfect gift for little bookworms who want to be transported to a world of magic. Turn any read-aloud evening into an unforgettable experience by discovering the stories from this e-book together with your

1. https://books2read.com/u/bPNk87

2. https://books2read.com/u/bPNk87

children. Let your kids immerse themselves in a world of adventure and fun and watch them fall asleep peacefully each night.